THE 20TH CENTURY
Upper Elementary Level
30 Pieces by Bartók, Bolcom, Dello Joio,
Kabalevsky, Shostakovich and Others
in Progressive Order

Compiled and Edited by Richard Walters

On the cover:
"The Horse, the Rider and the Clown", plate V of the illustrated book "Jazz"
by Henri Matisse (1869–1954).
Published by Editions Tériade, 1947.
© 2015 Succession H. Matisse / Artists Rights Society (ARS), New York

Image source: Archives H. Matisse

ISBN 978-1-4950-1022-4

G. SCHIRMER, Inc.

DISTRIBUTED BY
HAL•LEONARD®
CORPORATION
7777 W. BLUEMOUND RD. P.O. BOX 13819 MILWAUKEE, WI 53213

www.musicsalesclassical.com
www.halleonard.com

CONTENTS

Though the table of contents appears in alphabetical order by composer, the music in this book is in progressive order.

COMPOSER BIOGRAPHIES, HISTORICAL NOTES

AND

PRACTICE AND PERFORMANCE TIPS

The pieces in this collection are by some of the greatest composers of the 20th century, composers who wrote a full range of music for orchestra, voices, piano, and chamber ensembles, in the great and large forms. But they also valued music education, and composed interesting music to foster a student pianist's progress. The music by these composers leads a student not only to technical proficiency, but also to become a more fully formed, imaginative musician. Some of these pieces challenge a student to broaden experience beyond conventional, traditional harmony and rhythm. In these works a piano student gets a glimpse into the mind of a great, forward-thinking artistic genius.

In the 20th century composers generally conceived every detail in a composition (unless it is left to chance by design). Many students do not seem to understand the organic role that slurs, phrases, staccatos, accents, dynamics, pedaling, and changes of tempo play in a 20th century composition. Tempo, articulation and dynamics are in mind from the outset of composition, as essential to the music as are the notes and rhythms.

In earlier centuries it was not the custom for the composer to necessarily notate all articulation and pedaling. Insightful understanding of period style of playing informs many of these details in music from the Baroque and Classical eras. Even in music of the 19th century composers did not always notate all such details, and a player's understanding of style is necessary in adding things implied but not stated in the score. Most composers of the 20th century became much more specific about notating such matters. Almost without exception, articulations and dynamics are not editorial suggestions in *The 20th Century* series. They are by the composer and part of the composition. If

editorial suggestions are very occasionally made, they are specifically noted on a piece or indicated in brackets.

Pedaling in *The 20th Century* series is by the composer unless indicated otherwise on an individual piece. Fingering is also often by the composer. Metronome indications without brackets are by the composer. In works where the composer did not provide a suggested metronome indication, those in brackets are editorial suggestions.

The "Practice and Performance Tips" point out a few ideas that may be helpful to the student in learning a piece. These might also be used by a busy teacher as an at-a-glance look at some topics in teaching a piece.

The pieces as part of sets for "children" are actually for progressing pianists of any age. Composers needed a way to indicate to the world that the pieces were written for a contained level of difficulty and for students, and were to be thought of differently from concert works such as a sonata or concerto, for example. The tradition of titling these with some variation along the lines of a "children's album" was a convenient way of solving this. It has always been understood, and certainly by the composers themselves, that this music is about the level of the pianist, not the age of the pianist.

When a great talent turns attention to writing a short piece of limited difficulty level for students, it is approached with the same aesthetics, temperament, tastes and creative invention applied when composing a symphony, opera or concerto. These exquisite miniatures are complete works of timeless art. Through them a master musician of the past indirectly teaches a progressing musician of the present and the future.

BÉLA BARTÓK
(1881–1945, Hungarian; became a US citizen in 1945)

Béla Bartók is one of the most important and often performed composers of the twentieth century, and much of his music, including *Concerto for Orchestra*, his concertos, his string quartets, and his opera *Bluebeard's Castle*, holds a venerable position in the classical repertoire. His parents were amateur musicians who nurtured their young son with exposure to dance music, drumming, and piano lessons. In 1899 he started piano and composition studies at the Academy of Music in Budapest and not long after graduation he joined the Academy's piano faculty. Bartók wished to create music that was truly Hungarian at its core, a desire that sparked his deep interest in folk music. His work collecting and studying folksongs from around the Baltic region impacted his own compositional style greatly in terms of rhythm, mood, and texture. Bartók utilized folk influences to create a truly unique style. Though he composed opera, concertos, ballets, and chamber music, he was also committed to music education and composed several piano works for students, including his method *Mikrokosmos*. Bartók toured extensively in the 1920s and '30s, and became as well-known as both a pianist and composer. He immigrated to the US in 1940 to escape war and political turmoil in Europe, and settled in New York City, though the last years of his life were difficult, with many health problems.

Selections from *The First Term at the Piano*, Sz. 53, BB 66 (composed 1913)
With the original Hungarian title *Kezdők zongoramuzsikája*, these short pieces were selected from the 44 pieces Bartók composed for a piano method by Bartók and Sándor Reschofsky, published in 1913. The pieces were composed for piano students at Reschofsky's music school in Budapest. Some of the pieces are based on folksongs, others are original compositions. Fingerings, articulation and metronomic markings are by Bartók. After a series of setbacks and disappointments Bartók composed little in the years 1912–1914. His international acclaim and successful concert tours lay ahead, in the 1920s. The little pieces in *The First Term at the Piano* were the great composer's only compositions in 1913. In the previous year, 1912, Bartók prepared teaching editions of Bach, Beethoven, Haydn and Mozart which became standard pedagogical publications in Hungary.

Crescendos
Practice and Performance Tips
- Note the title of the piece, and the crescendo markings the composer has created.
- Obviously, Bartók thought playing the crescendo as written was essential to the piece.
- Practice slowly hands separately.

- Aim for evenness of volume and tone, smoothness in moving from note to note, and steadiness of tempo.
- Bartók has written several specific dynamics and articulations. Pay attention!
- The phrasing, sometimes ending with a slur to a staccato note, is essential to the music.
- Use no pedal at all.

Folksong
Practice and Performance Tips
- Tempo is always relative. Though Bartók has written that the quarter note = 52 (which is quite slow), he has also written *Moderato*. The composer knew that for a student pianist this would feel moderate, not slow.
- The left hand is an accompaniment to the right-hand melody throughout.
- Practice the left hand separately.
- As you practice the left hand alone, work on a smooth motion (indicated by the two-measure phrase mark).
- The composer has asked the pianist to play the left-hand figure smoothly at both f and p.
- The right-hand melody needs close attention to phrasing, staccato and dynamics.
- The dynamic changes from f to p and back to f happen suddenly, without a gradual increase or decrease.
- Use no pedal at all.

Hungarian Folk Song
Practice and Performance Tips
- The tempo *Allegro* and the metronome suggestion (by Bartók) are relative and for students, not a true *allegro*. Do not try to take the tempo too quickly.
- Practice hands separately.
- Attempt to create a smooth and even motion in the left hand, which is an accompaniment to the right hand in this piece.
- Bartók, who understood progressing pianists, allows the student to master this accompaniment figure playing f, rather than asking for subtlety.
- Note the phrasing as you practice the left hand alone.
- The right-hand melody needs to be played with a singing tone. Note the composer's phrasing.
- This piece could be played with no pedal at all.
- If pedal is used, it should change when the harmony in the left hand changes.

Walking
Practice and Performance Tips
- In giving right and left hands different dynamics, the composer is encouraging independence of the hands.
- Practice each hand separately at first, playing the dynamic as composed.
- Playing left hand f and right hand p, then switching (in measure 5) requires coordination and concentration. This will take quite a bit of practice for most students.

- Notice from the phrase markings that the entire piece is played smoothly, no matter whether f or p.
- Keep a steady tempo, in the spirit of the even stride of walking.
- Do not use pedal.

Selections from *For Children*, Sz. 42, BB 53
(composed 1908–09)

Bartók was one of the pioneering ethnomusicologists in eastern Europe, collecting and documenting thousands of folksongs from Hungary and neighboring countries. The original edition of *For Children* was in four volumes. Volumes 1–2 were compositions based on Hungarian folk songs. Volumes 3–4 were compositions based on Slovakian folk songs. Bartók created a revised edition in 1943, with fairly minor changes to the original regarding compositional content, with the pieces retitled. Some pieces were eliminated for the revised edition, and the four volumes were consolidated into two.

Children's Song (Volume 1)

From Volume 1 of the original four volume edition, with the English title "The Sun Is Out." Bartók changed the title for the revised edition.

Practice and Performance Tips
- Do not play this lovely, simple piece too quickly.
- Practice hands separately first, learning all the accents, slurs and phrases and dynamics as you learn the notes and rhythms.
- Capture the gentle spirit of this music.
- Play with a quiet touch, with crescendos blooming up from p only in a few spots.
- In measures 18–20 experiment with a very slight lift at the end of each slur.
- Use no pedal except where Bartók has indicated, in the last three measures.

Happy Thoughts (Volume 1)

From Volume 1 in the original four volume edition. The title in English, "Happy Thoughts" comes from the original edition. The piece is untitled (No. 15) in the revised edition.

Practice and Performance Tips
- *Grazioso* means graceful and pretty. Even though the piece is rhythmic and with frequent staccato, refrain from playing it aggressively.
- Practice hands separately first, learning all the accents, slurs and phrases and dynamics as you learn the notes and rhythms.
- When practicing the staccato left-hand chords, make sure all the notes are evenly and crisply played.
- Play the slurred staccato notes marked *poco sosten.* as slightly separated, different than true short staccato.

- The *ritard.* in measures 11–2 and 19–20, followed by a return to the tempo, are playful touches.
- Use no pedal at all.

Sorrow (Volume 2)

From Volume 3 of the original four volume edition, with the English title "Song of the Vagabond." Bartók changed the title for the revised edition.

Practice and Performance Tips
- The right hand plays the sad melody, accompaniment by the left hand.
- Practice the right hand alone, carefully shaping the phrasing as indicated, and conjuring the sweet sadness in it.
- Practice the left hand alone, smoothly moving from chord to chord, and slurring each measure as composed.
- Then practice hands together slowly, retaining the phrasing from the hands alone practice.
- The short descrescendo, which happens frequently, is a traditional musical device that implies weeping.
- Play all phrasing clearly, as composed, and without pedal. Pedal likely would blur the careful structure.

WILLIAM BOLCOM
(b. 1938, American)

William Bolcom is one of the most successful American composers of the late 20th century. He was born in Seattle, Washington, and studied composition with Darius Milhaud, Olivier Messiaen, and Leland Smith. Early in his career he wrote serialist music, influenced by Boulez, Berio, and Stockhausen, but he eventually began to incorporate more popular styles into his works in order to blur the lines between art music and popular music. He has written eight symphonies, three operas (performed at Lyric Opera of Chicago, the Metropolitan Opera and other major houses), as well as numerous concertos, quartets, sonatas, concert piano works and piano rags, art songs and cabaret-style songs. His compositions have won many awards, including the Pulitzer Prize and two Grammy Awards. As a pianist, he has recorded works by Milhaud, Gershwin, and himself, as well as some twenty albums with his wife, mezzo-soprano Joan Morris.

Selections from *Monsterpieces (and Others)*
(composed 1980)

The ten pieces in this set are designated "for older children." The original publication (still available) includes drawings and brief pedagogical notes from the composer. These pieces were premiered not by a child, but by Joan Morris, Bolcom's wife, when she was studying piano.

The Bad Mister

Practice and Performance Tips

- Bolcom explores the lower range of the piano in this piece.
- Clarity in playing becomes especially important in this range.
- As the composer states, "very little pedal." Maybe none!
- The melody in the left hand is slightly louder than the accompaniment in the right hand.
- Practice the left hand separately, carefully observing the composer's slurring, staccato markings, accents, and dynamics.
- Make sure the staccato chords in the right hand are played crisply and cleanly, with all the notes sounding evenly and at the same time.
- Keep the right-hand chords staccato throughout; do not let the articulation get lazy.

Badminton

Practice and Performance Tips

- This is composed with no meter, a common 20th century composition technique.
- The composer asks for *una corda*, the soft pedal, to be held throughout.
- Everything is staccato, indicated by the composer's marking *sempre* (always) over the staccato near the beginning.
- Imagine a badminton game. Each hand represents a player hitting the shuttlecock over the net.
- This can be any tempo, but it should not be played more quickly than the pace of a badminton game.
- A badminton shuttlecock makes a soft sound when hitting the racket or the ground, indicated by *pp*.
- The winning shot in each line is emphasized with *sfz* (or on line three, the first *sfz* is an attempted winning shot).
- In this *pp* context the *sfz* is not a sudden *fff*. Think of it more like *mp*.
- A pianist needs to find the fun in playing this unconventional piece.
- You should be a bit of an actor in portraying this badminton game at the piano.

The Plaid Miss

Practice and Performance Tips

- Bolcom introduces the student to a few concepts in this brief piece. The term definitions are from the composer.
- Practice hands separately, and as the composer states, play as smoothly as possible without using pedal.
- The composer has asked for many specific dynamics, covering a large range. Pay careful attention!
- Take care to shape the music using the phrasing indicated.
- This quirky little piece has an air of charming melancholy. Play it gracefully.

NORMAN DELLO JOIO
(1913–2008, American)

One of the most notable American composers in mid-20th century, Norman Dello Joio grew up in a musical home in New York City, the son of an Italian immigrant father who worked as an organist, pianist, singer, and vocal coach. Musicians were constantly in the home, including singers from the Metropolitan Opera who came for coaching sessions. Norman took organ lessons from his godfather, Pietro Yon (composer of the Christmas classic "Gesù Bambino"), a composer and the organist for St. Patrick's Cathedral in New York. He worked as an organist in his teens, before deciding to turn his attention to composition instead. After initial composition study at the Institute of Musical Art and the Juilliard School, Dello Joio began studying with Paul Hindemith at the Yale School of Music. Hindemith encouraged Dello Joio to embrace the natural tonal lyricism of his writing (as opposed to the atonality then in vogue), which was infused with the spirit of Italian opera and the church music of his childhood, as well as early jazz. Dello Joio remained true to his style in writing operas, ballets, orchestral pieces, solo instrumental works, art songs, piano music, and choral music. He was on the faculties of Sarah Lawrence College, the Mannes College of Music, and Boston University. In 1957, the Young Composers Project, which placed composers under the age of thirty-five as composers-in-residence of public high schools around the country, was founded based upon Dello Joio's suggestion.

Selections from *Suite for the Young*
(composed 1964)

Dello Joio's constant work as a teacher in various capacities allowed him insight into writing music intended for students, some of which is for piano. Other piano works for students include the *Suite for Piano* and *Prelude: To a Young Musician*. *Suite for the Young* is the only music for piano Dello Joio wrote for the first or second year piano student.

Little Sister

Practice and Performance Tips

- Play smoothly and tenderly, without pedal.
- Practice hands separately.
- In the left hand practice sustaining a note while playing another note.
- The above happens first in the first four measures, then in a different pattern beginning in measure 9.
- The right hand is a melody that needs to be played in a singing tone, and slightly louder than the left-hand accompaniment.
- Play with no pedal.

Mountain Melody

Practice and Performance Tips

- The piece has the feel of a simple folk tune, made interesting by Dello Joio's harmonization.
- Notice the indication legato, and the composer's phrase markings.
- The melody begins in the right hand, then is almost exactly repeated an octave lower in the left hand.
- Note the rather dramatic dynamic changes, including the sudden shift to *mf* in measures 5 and 8.
- Even with the strong dynamic contrasts this piece needs to be played with a gentleness of spirit.
- Use no pedal. Create the smoothness of this music with the fingers only.
- A slight *rit.* is possible in the last two measures.

DAVID DIAMOND

(1915–2005, American)

David Diamond was born in Rochester, NY, to Austrian and Polish parents. He studied at the Cleveland Institute of Music and the Eastman School of Music, then with Roger Sessions at the New School in New York before traveling to Paris to study with Nadia Boulanger. A Guggenheim Fellowship allowed him to remain in Paris until the outbreak of World War II. Diamond and the neo-classicists held a different view from the atonalists in fashion in mid-century. "We've composed music that we find beautiful, that we have loved," he said. "You have to write music that will be loved. Now if that's a sentimental concept of what being a composer is, then I'm very sorry."[1] Although the upward trajectory of his career tapered off, he remained part of the New York scene. In 1966, he conducted the premiere of his Piano Concerto with the New York Philharmonic. Leonard Bernstein, who advocated for Diamond's works, conducted the premiere of his Fifth Symphony on the same program. From 1973–1986 he was professor of composition at the Juilliard School of Music. He continued to teach there following his retirement until 1997. Interest in his works revived in the 1980s and 1990s, and he won the Gold Medal of the American Academy of Arts and Letters and an Edward MacDowell in 1991, as well as President Bill Clinton's National Medal of Arts in 1995.

[1] Daniel J. Wakin, *David Diamond, 89, Intensely Lyrical Composer, Is Dead*, New York Times, June 15, 2005, accessed October 6, 2014 http://www.nytimes.com/2005/06/15/arts/music/15diamond.html.

Selections from *Eight Piano Pieces*

(composed 1940)

Diamond wrote two piano sonatas, two piano sonatinas, five preludes and fugue for piano, and a few other works for the instrument. His *Eight Piano Pieces, Album for the Young* and *Then and Now* are his works for piano students.

The *Eight Piano Pieces* were inspired by nursery rhymes, children's songs, and other images from childhood.

Jumping Jacks

Practice and Performance Tips

- This brief piece introduces imitation between the hands, with the right hand leading.
- Practice slowly hands separately, learning the staccato markings and accents as you learn the notes and rhythms.
- Then move to practicing hands together slowly, retaining all the articulation learned with hands separately.
- Play the chords marked with a tenuto (−) with slight separation.
- Make the most of the dramatic changes in dynamics, from *p* to *f*.
- Use no pedal at all.

Pease-Porridge Hot

Practice and Performance Tips

- Diamond's short piece has the spirit of a modal old English tune.
- The challenge to the progressing pianist is the multi-note chords.
- Highlight the contrast between the legato phrase in measures 1–2, 5–6, 9–10 with the chords in measures 3–4 and 7–8.
- Play the chords marked with a tenuto (−) with slight separation.
- The most complex spot is measure 12, when notes are added to the chords. A *rallentando* helps to make this ending both graceful and powerful.
- No pedal is recommended until measures 11–12.

MORTON GOULD

(1913–1996, American)

Morton Gould was born in Queens to an Australian father and a Russian mother. He composed his first work, a waltz for piano, when he was six. At eight he entered the Institute of Musical Art, which would later become the Juilliard School. His first work was published by G. Schirmer in 1932 when he was eighteen. Gould was a distinctly American presence, writing in both popular and contemporary classical styles and proving himself adept at conquering the rising mediums of radio and cinema. In the 1930s he played piano in vaudeville acts and at cinemas and dance studies. For radio he composed commercial jingles and radio symphonettes, and he also worked as a conductor, arranger, and composer for WOR New York's weekly "Music for Today" program. In 1933, Stokowski premiered his *Chorale and Fugue in Jazz* with the Philadelphia Orchestra. Gould wrote in various styles and blurred the lines between classical and popular music. Besides concert works he also wrote for Broadway. His works were performed by the New York Philharmonic, the Cleveland Orchestra other leading orchestras. In 1994 he was awarded a Kennedy Center Honor for his contributions to American culture, and in 1995 he won the Pulitzer Prize for his final orchestral work, *Stringmusic*, which he wrote on commission for the National Symphony Orchestra as a farewell to Mstislav Rostropovich.

Both *At the Piano* (Books 1 and 2) and *Ten for Deborah* were written for Gould's daughter Deborah as she studied piano.

The Missing Beat! from *At the Piano*, Book 1
(composed 1964)
Practice and Performance Tips
- Begin practice slowly, hands together, learning the articulation, accents and dynamics as you learn the notes and rhythms.
- Keep a steady beat in this happy waltz. If the beat is not steady the "joke" of the missing beat will be lost.
- Play with a light and buoyant touch.
- Do not rush through the full measure of rest in measures 20 and 40.
- Use no pedal, keeping the music crisp and clear.

Loud and Soft from *Ten for Deborah*
(composed 1964)
Practice and Performance Tips
- The 7/4 measure is divided in to 4 beats + 3 beats throughout, indicated with a dotted bar line.
- Articulation has been carefully composed, with staccato markings, slurs, accents and pedaling.
- Learn the articulation as you learn the notes and rhythms, not added later.
- Practice should begin at a slow tempo. Gradually increase the speed as you master the music, but always keep a steady beat, whatever the tempo.
- Use pedal only in the spots Gould has composed, and only exactly as indicated.
- It is very important to point up the sharp contrasts in dynamics, especially in a piece titled "Loud and Soft!"

DMITRI KABALEVSKY
(1904–1987, Russian)

Kabalevsky was an important Russian composer of the Soviet era who wrote music in many genres, including four symphonies, a handful of operas, theatre and film scores, patriotic music, choral music, vocal music, and numerous piano works. He embraced the Soviet notion of socialist realism in art, a fact that was more than politically advantageous to his career in the USSR. While studying piano and composition at the Moscow Conservatory, he taught piano lessons at a music college and it was for these students that he began writing works for young players. In 1932 he began teaching at the Moscow Conservatory, earning the title of professor in 1939. He eventually went on to develop programs for the concert hall, radio, and television aimed at teaching children about classical music. In the last decades of his life, Kabalevsky focused on developing music curricula for schools, retiring from the Moscow Conservatory to teach in public schools where he could test his theories and the effectiveness of his syllabi. This he considered his true life's work, and his pedagogical principles revolutionized music education in Russia. A collection of his writings on music education was published in English in 1988 as *Music and Education: A Composer Writes About Musical Education.*

Selections from *30 Pieces for Children*, Op. 27
(composed 1937–38)
Kabalevsky often quoted Maxim Gorki, saying that books for children should be "the same as for adults, only better." Kabalevsky believed strongly in writing music for young players that was not dumbed-down, but rather, complete, imaginative compositions unto themselves. Kabalevsky did a slight revision of Op. 27 in 1985, which was intended to be an authoritative edition. (This is our source for the pieces in this collection.)

Waltz, Op. 27, No. 1
Practice and Performance Tips
- The quiet, treble range of the piece reminds one of a music box.
- Feel the tempo in whole measures with the lilt of a waltz, rather than individual beats.
- Practice hands together slowly.
- The entire piece is built on two-note slurs. These should be played cleanly and gracefully.
- In the right hand the two-note slur ends in a sustained quarter note. Do not clip this quarter note too short, which would destroy the *cantabile* of the right-hand melody.
- In the left hand the two-note slur ends on an eighth note; gently release this quickly.
- Kabalevsky deliberately introduces students to a double sharp in measure 14.
- Make the most of the dynamic contrasts.

A Little Song, Op. 27, No. 2
Practice and Performance Tips
- Do not take this rather sad piece too quickly, which would destroy its mood and essence.
- Practice hands separately, observing carefully the phrasing the composer has indicated.
- The melody is passed from hand to hand, beginning in the right hand.
- The melody should be slightly more prominent than the accompanying hand.
- The composer's marking of *dolce* should be respected; play this piece gently, with sweetness.
- Create the drama the composer intended by

playing all the dynamic contrasts.
- The most dramatic moment is the move from f in measure 12 to *subito p* in measure 13.
- Use no pedal at all.

Selections from *24 Pieces for Children*, Op. 39 (composed 1944)

Kabalevsky began writing piano music for students as early as 1927. His first major set, *30 Children's Pieces* of Op. 27, was composed in 1937–38. The *24 Pieces for Children* (alternately titled *24 Easy Pieces*) of Op. 39 is for an earlier level of study than Op. 27. Though Kabalevsky composed operas, orchestral music, concertos and chamber music throughout his career, as well as more difficult piano literature, he returned to writing music for piano students periodically in his life, reflecting his deeply felt commitment to music education.

Waltz, Op. 39, No. 13
Practice and Performance Tips
- Throughout the right hand plays a melody, accompanied by the left hand.
- Practice the right hand alone to create a beautiful and flowing melody, playing smoothly, noticing the composer's phrasing.
- If played without phrase structure, this melody will not be what Kabalevsky composed.
- Also practice the left hand separately, keeping this simple accompaniment gentle and quiet.
- With hands together, let the melody in the right hand be slightly louder than the accompaniment in the left hand.
- Play this lovely, melancholy waltz with no pedal.

Jumping, Op. 39, No. 15
Practice and Performance Tips
- The piece is almost hands in octaves throughout, but with the composer's brilliant and simple twist of delaying the first beat in one hand by half a beat.
- The left hand leads in measures 1–8 and measures 17–23. The right hand leads in measures 9–16.
- The trickiest spot is measure 9, when the lead switches to the right hand.
- The articulation is key to successfully playing "Jumping."
- Throughout, the notes of beat 1 are slurred to a staccato on beat 2, followed by a staccato on beat 3.
- Note the sudden change to p in measure 9, followed the crescendo beginning in measure 15.
- The tempo and the title of the piece are clear indications of its fun spirit.
- Use no pedal at all.

Folk Dance, Op. 39, No. 17
Practice and Performance Tips
- Even though the hands play together in thirds and not octaves, they play the same rhythms and

articulations together throughout.
- Begin by practicing each hand separately and slowly.
- Learn the articulation (staccato markings, accents and slurs) and dynamics from the beginning, as you are learning the notes and rhythms.
- Then practice hands together slowly, retaining the articulation and dynamics already learned when hands were practiced separately.
- Over time, increase the speed of your practice, keeping a steady beat throughout.
- A worthy aim is a buoyant, light touch, even when playing at f.
- Use no pedal. Pedaling would spoil the crisp texture of the music.
- The end result should sound happy and carefree, not labored.

Clowns, Op. 39, No. 20
Practice and Performance Tips
- Begin practice hands separately and slowly.
- Learn the articulation (slurs, staccato, accents) as you learn the notes and rhythms.
- Learning the articulation from the beginning will help you learn the notes and rhythms.
- The melody is in the right hand, played with slight prominence over the left hand.
- The left-hand staccato notes should be played with a light bounce.
- Exactly and crisply playing the slurs, staccato, accents and dynamics will convey the fun shenanigans of circus clowns.
- Use no pedal at all.

Selections from *35 Easy Pieces*, Op. 89 (composed 1972–74)

Kabalevsky's last large set of piano pieces for students was composed in his late sixties, after a lifetime of experiences with young musicians, and after he had attained a revered position as the cultural leader of music education in the USSR. These were also his last compositions for piano. After 1974 Kabalevsky only wrote a few more compositions, which were songs or small choral pieces.

The Shrew, Op. 89, No. 12
Practice and Performance Tips
- Kabalevsky is teaching the student about enharmonic spelling of notes in this piece.
- Enharmonics means that the same note is notated different ways. For instance, B-flat or A-sharp.
- Left and right hands play the same notes in octaves throughout.
- Most measures are comprised of an accented half note slurred to a short eighth note.
- Learn and accomplish the articulation with the fingers only before using the pedaling Kabalevsky has composed.

- When using the pedaling, be sure to release exactly as you play the eighth note on beat 3.
- This is a character piece, in this case a portrait of a strident, hot tempered woman (a shrew).

Little Goat Limping, Op. 89, No. 19
Practice and Performance Tips
- For this piece in 5/4, the composer has helped by putting in dotted bar lines to divide the measure into two groups: 3 beats + 2 beats.
- Find the natural lilt in this music in 5/4, with a stronger emphasis on beat 1, followed by a lighter emphasis on beat 4.
- Executing the slurs and accents as Kabalevsky composed them will create the character of the piece.
- We suggest playing beats 3 and 5 in the right hand in measures 1–3 with separation just short of true staccato.
- Notice how the composer decorates the melody a bit when the music from measures 1–4 returns in measures 9–12, with different slurring the second time.
- Use no pedal in this crisply rhythmic piece.

The Little Harpist, Op. 89, No. 24
Practice and Performance Tips
- As the title indicates, this music imitates a harp.
- It is crucial to play the composer's phrasing, passing the phrase from hand to hand.
- A traditional technical approach would be to practice slowly, deliberately playing *non legato*, making each sixteenth note very even.
- Follow the above by playing smoothly and elegantly, but attempting to retain the evenness of the sixteenth notes.
- As the music is mastered, the tempo can increase.
- Practice without pedal. Kabalevsky (who often indicated pedaling in his piano music) did not mark any pedaling, a strong clue that he intended this little piece to be played without pedal.

Stubborn Little Brother, Op. 89, No. 27
Practice and Performance Tips
- The wit of this adorable piece comes from someone attempting to persuade sweetly, with a blunt response that refuses to comply.
- Through most of the piece (except for measures 18–20) the right hand plays smoothly and the left hand plays with strong *marcato* accents.
- Practice slowly hands together.
- The pedaling is by the composer. Pedal exactly as he wrote it, using pedal nowhere else.
- Be sure to release the pedal cleanly, exactly in the spot the composer indicates.
- Typical of Kabalevsky, the piece has many intricate details of articulation, slurring, dynamics and pedaling, all composed along with the notes.

OCTAVIO PINTO
(1890–1950, Brazilian)

Octavio Pinto was born in Sao Paulo, Brazil. Pinto enjoyed a successful career as an architect, but he was also an avid music lover, a skillful composer and pianist, and was well-connected to musical life in Brazil. In 1922 he married the famous piano virtuoso Gulomar Novaes, and he was also a close friend of composer Heitor Villa-Lobos. He took lessons for a time from Isidore Philipp, but it was mostly as a composer that his love and talent for music expressed itself throughout his life. He composed piano music, generally character pieces in nature or showpieces, until his death. His most well-known and oft-played work is *Scenas Infantis* (Memories of Childhood) of 1932, which became a signature piece performed by Novaes.

Minuet from *Children's Festival: Little Suite for the Piano* (composed 1939)
Practice and Performance Tips
- The composer has composed a minuet deliberately reminiscent of the 18th century.
- This minuet should be played in a style similar to a minuet by Mozart.
- Play gracefully, cleanly and evenly, using no sustaining pedal.
- The two-note slur on beats 1 and 2 followed by a shorter note on beat 3 (such as in right hand measures 1 and 2) is essential to the classic minuet style.
- The quick decrescendo in measure 16 to the soft return of the main theme in measure 17 is a magical moment.
- The grace notes in measure 25 are played slightly before the principal note, with the principal note occurring on beat 3.

DMITRI SHOSTAKOVICH
(1906–1975, Russian)

A major mid-20th century composer, Shostakovich is famous for his epic symphonies, concertos, operas, string quartets, and other chamber works. Born in St. Petersburg, his entire career took place in Soviet-era Russia. His life teetered between receiving high official honors and living with an almost debilitating fear of arrest for works that did not adhere to the Soviet ideals of socialist realism. In 1934, his opera *Lady Macbeth of the Mtsensk District* met with great popular success, but was banned by Stalin for the next thirty years as modernist, surrealist, and obscene. The following year, Stalin began a campaign known as the Purges, executing or exiling to prison camps politicians, intellectuals and artists. Shostakovich managed to avoid such a fate, and despite an atmosphere of anxiety and repression was able to compose an astounding number of works with originality, humor, and emotional power. He succeeded in striking a balance between modernism and tradition that continues to make his music accessible to a broad audience. An excellent pianist, Shostakovich performed concertos by Mozart, Prokofiev, and Tchaikovsky early in his career, but after 1930 limited himself to performing his own works and some chamber music. He taught instrumentation and composition at the Leningrad Conservatory from 1937–1968, with brief breaks due to war and other political disruptions, and at the Moscow Conservatory in the 1940s. Since his death in 1975, Shostakovich has become one of the most performed 20th century composers.

Selections from *Children's Notebook for Piano*, Op. 69 (composed 1944–45)

Among a huge output of symphonies, operas and chamber music, Shostakovich wrote only a few pieces for piano students. *Children's Notebook for Piano* was written for his eight-year old daughter, Galina, for her studies on the instrument. The original set was published as six pieces. The seventh piece, "Birthday," written for Galina's ninth birthday in 1945, was added in a later edition.

The Bear, Op. 69, No. 3
Practice and Performance Tips
- The composer's indication of *non legato* applies to all the notes of the piece not marked with a slur.
- This light-hearted, comical piece seems to capture a bear at mischievous play, or maybe a circus bear.
- Practice hands separately first, applying the *non legato* touch and the marked slurs.
- The f sections should have a buoyant touch, even though playing loudly.

- Make the most of the sudden changes from f to p and back to f.
- Any sustaining pedal would spoil the crisp rhythm of this piece. Use no pedal at all.

Merry Tale, Op. 69, No. 4
Practice and Performance Tips
- Practice hands separately, first at a slow tempo.
- Learn the composer's articulation (staccato, tenuto accents, slurs) from the beginning, not added later.
- In measures 1–3 in the right hand, make a distinction between the staccato eighth notes and the tenuto quarter note.
- After hands alone practice, move to slow practice hands together, retaining the articulation you have already learned.
- This piece needs a crisp, light touch, even in f sections.
- Any sustaining pedal would completely spoil the texture of the music. Use no pedal.

Sad Tale, Op. 69, No. 5
Practice and Performance Tips
- The composer's marking of *legato sempre* indicates that the entire piece should be played smoothly.
- Begin practice slowly, hands separately.
- Strive for an evenness in tone in smoothly moving from note to note.
- The legato should be accomplished with the fingers. Use no pedal.
- Keep a steady beat throughout.

— Richard Walters, editor
Joshua Parman, Charmaine Siagian and Rachel Kelly, assistant editors

Jumping
from *24 Pieces for Children*

Dmitri Kabalevsky
Op. 39, No. 15

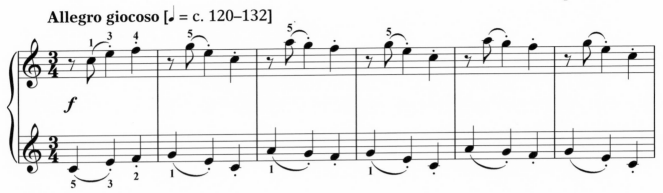

Fingerings are editorial suggestions.

Mountain Melody
from *Suite for the Young*

Norman Dello Joio

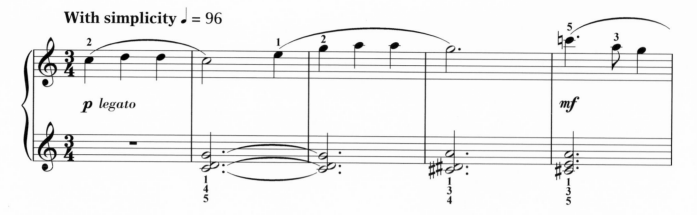

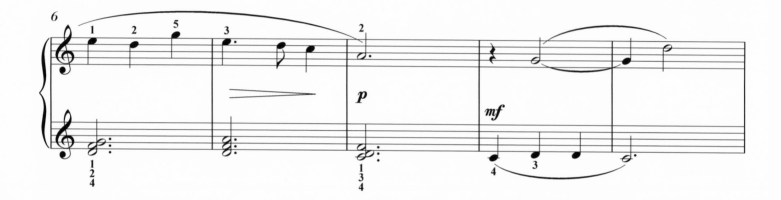

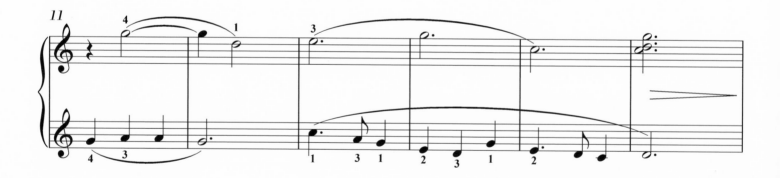

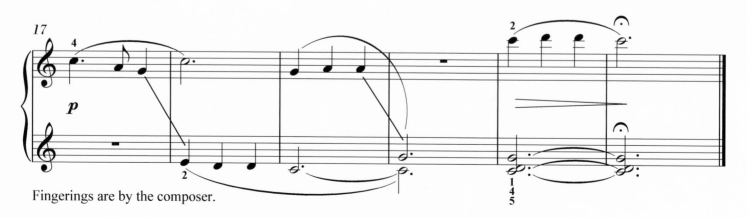

Fingerings are by the composer.

Hungarian Folksong
from *The First Term at the Piano*

Belá Bartók

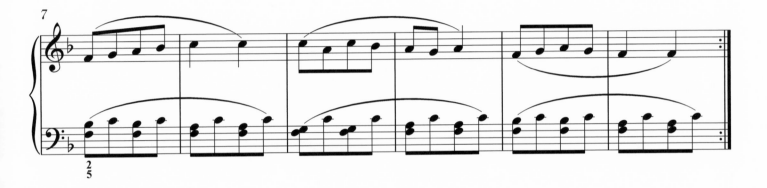

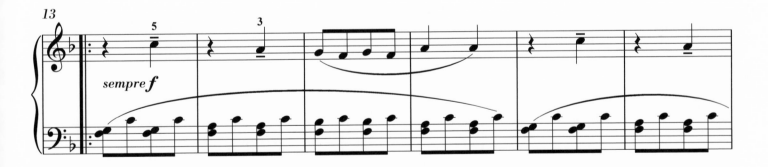

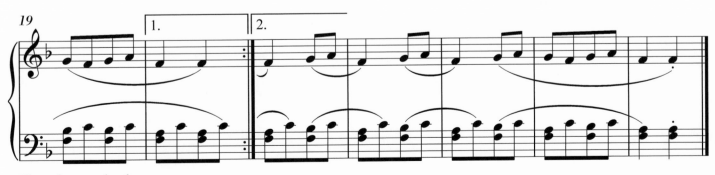

Fingerings are by the composer.

Waltz
from *24 Pieces for Children*

Dmitri Kabalevsky
Op. 39, No. 13

Moderato [♩ = c. 104–112]

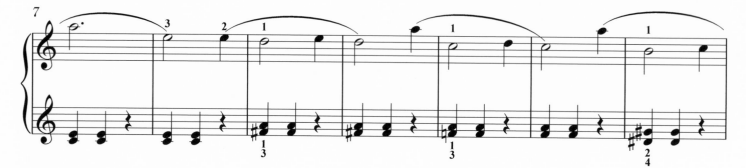

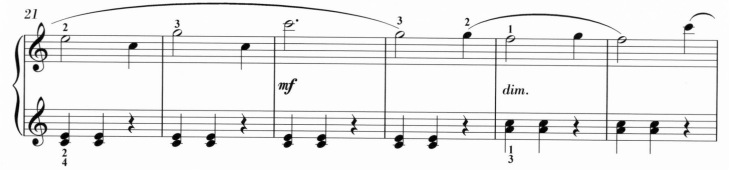

Fingerings are editorial suggestions.

Minuet
from *Children's Festival: Little Suite for the Piano*

Octavio Pinto

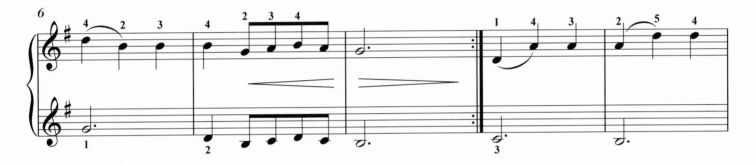

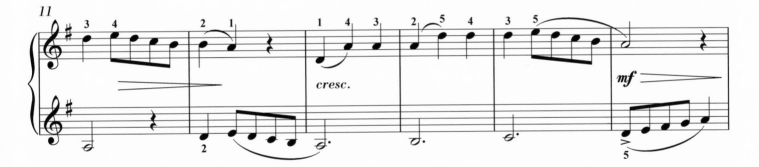

Fingerings are by the composer.

The Little Harpist
from *35 Easy Pieces*

Dmitri Kabalevsky
Op. 89, No. 24

Fingerings are by the composer.

Folksong
from *The First Term at the Piano*

Belá Bartók

Fingerings are by the composer.

Crescendos
from *The First Term at the Piano*

Belá Bartók

Fingerings are by the composer.

A Little Song
from *30 Pieces for Children*

Dmitri Kabalevsky
Op. 27, No. 2

Andantino [♩ = c. 80–88]

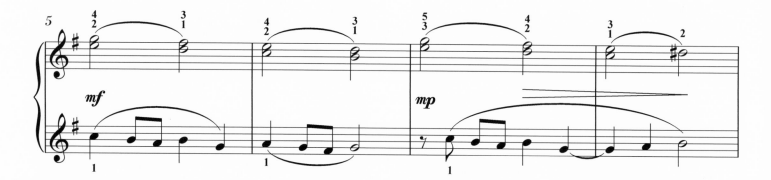

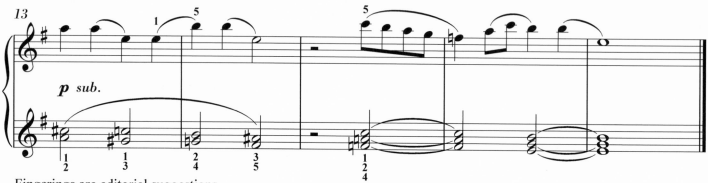

Fingerings are editorial suggestions.

Walking
from *The First Term at the Piano*

Belá Bartók

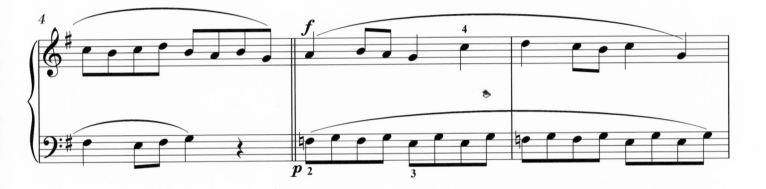

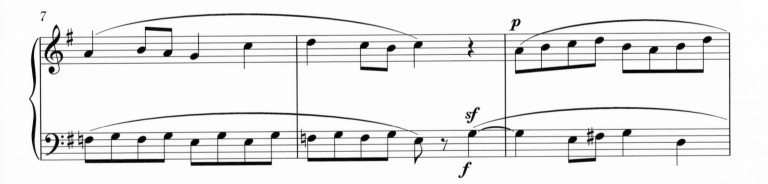

Fingerings are by the composer.

Waltz
from *30 Pieces for Children*

Dmitri Kabalevsky
Op. 27, No. 1

Allegretto cantabile [♩ = c. 108–120]

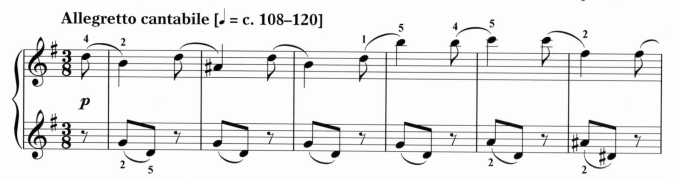

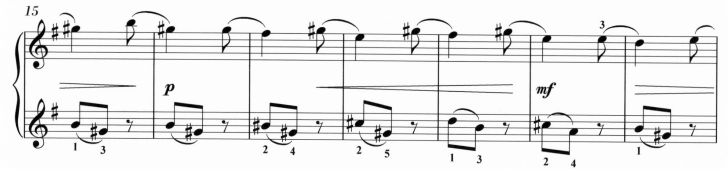

Fingerings are editorial suggestions.

Stubborn Little Brother
from *35 Easy Pieces*

Dmitri Kabalevsky
Op. 89, No. 27

Fingerings are by the composer.
*Use fingers 2 and 3.

Little Sister
from *Suite for the Young*

Norman Dello Joio

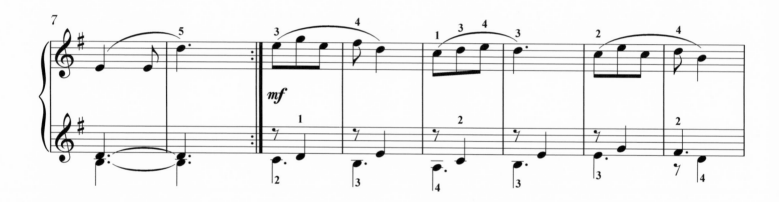

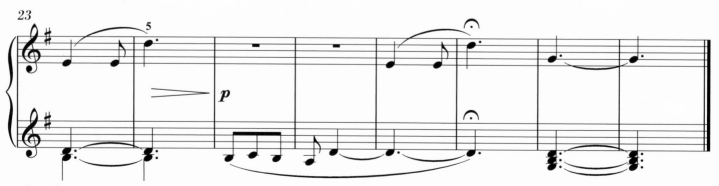

Fingerings are by the composer.

The Bad Mister

from *Monsterpieces (and Others)*

William Bolcom

Fingerings are by the composer.

Sorrow
from *For Children*, Volume 2

Belá Bartók

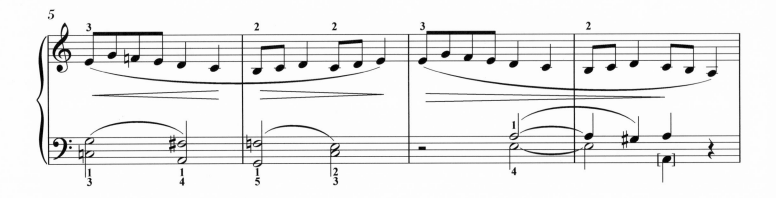

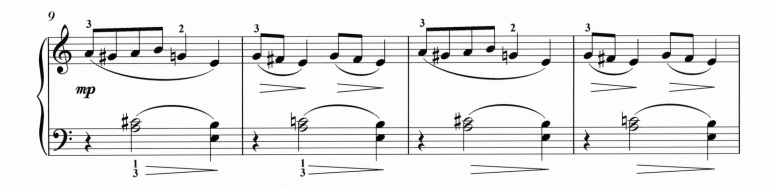

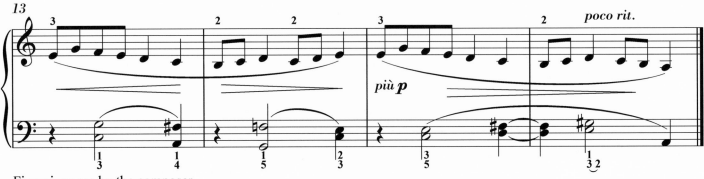

Fingerings are by the composer.

Children's Song
from *For Children*, Volume 1

Belá Bartók

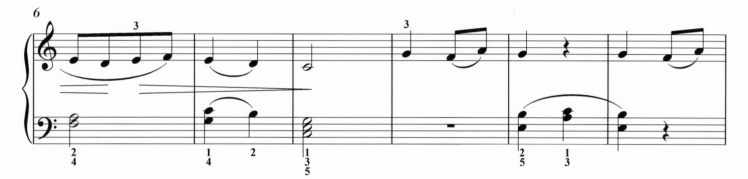

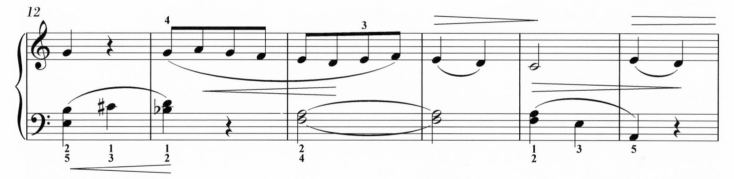

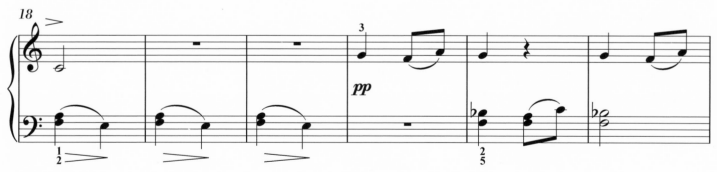

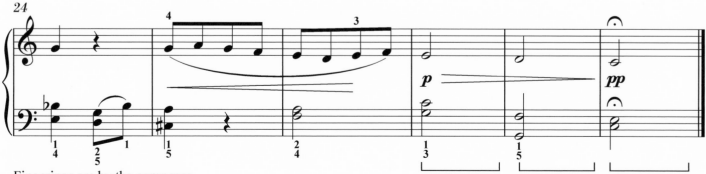

Fingerings are by the composer.

Pease-Porridge Hot
from *Eight Piano Pieces*

David Diamond

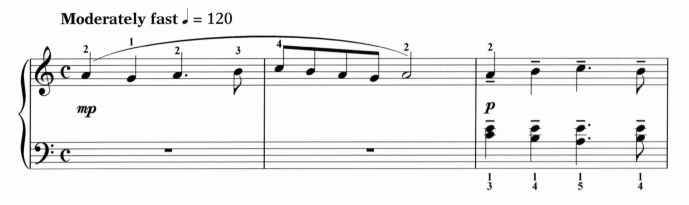

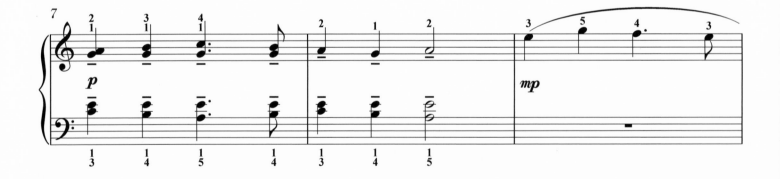

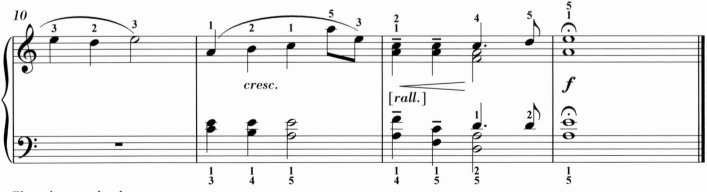

Fingerings are by the composer.

Jumping Jacks
from *Eight Piano Pieces*

David Diamond

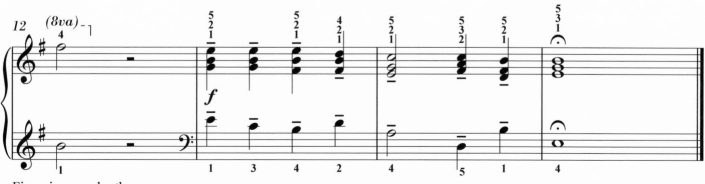

Fingerings are by the composer.

Folk Dance
from *24 Pieces for Children*

Dmitri Kabalevsky
Op. 39, No. 17

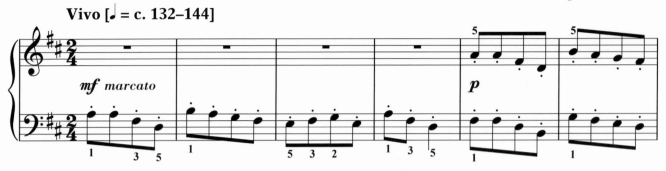

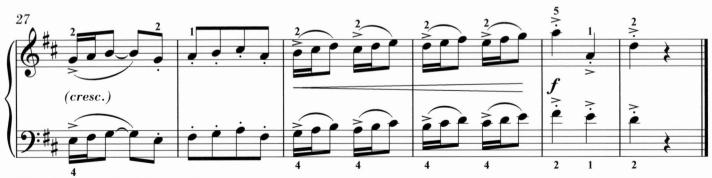

Fingerings are editorial suggestions.

Little Goat Limping
from *35 Easy Pieces*

Dmitri Kabalevsky
Op. 89, No. 19

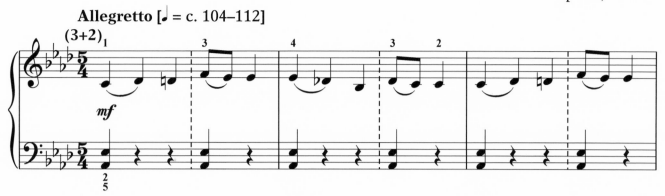

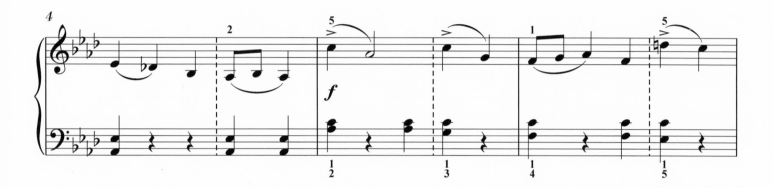

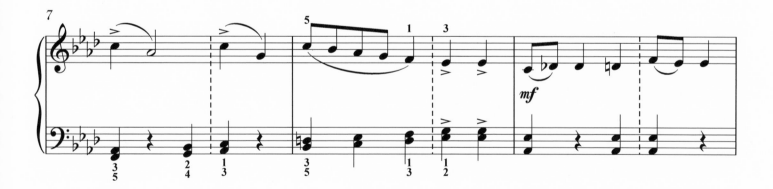

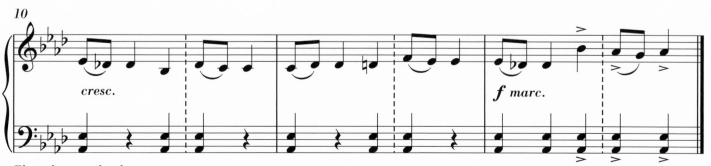

Fingerings are by the composer.

The Bear

from *Children's Notebook for Piano*

Dmitri Shostakovich
Op. 69, No. 3

Allegretto [♩ = c. 104–112]

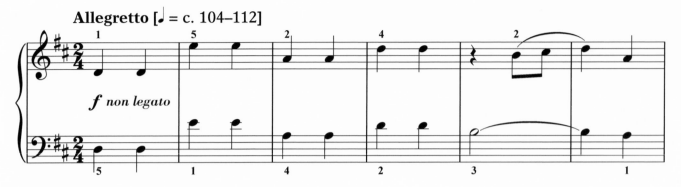

f non legato

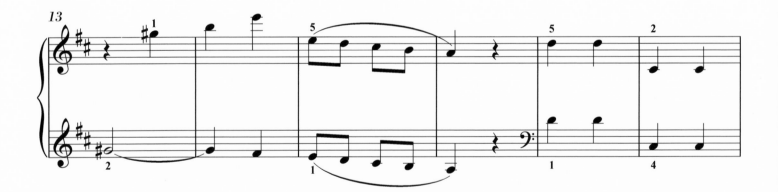

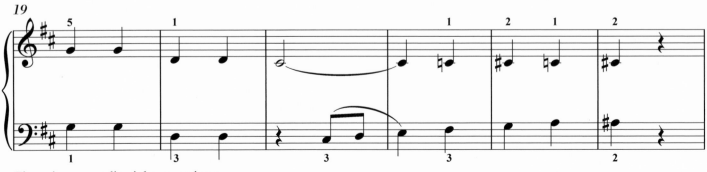

Fingerings are editorial suggestions.

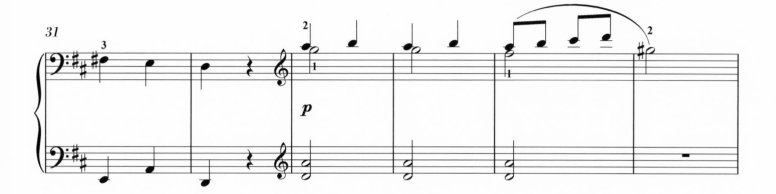

Happy Thoughts
from *For Children*, Volume 1

Belá Bartók

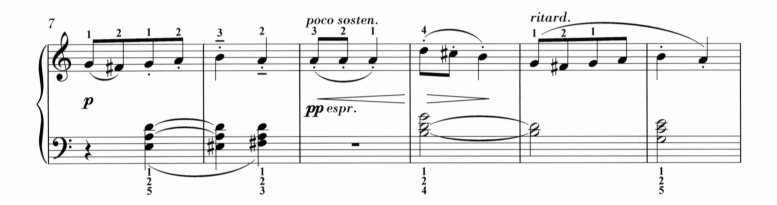

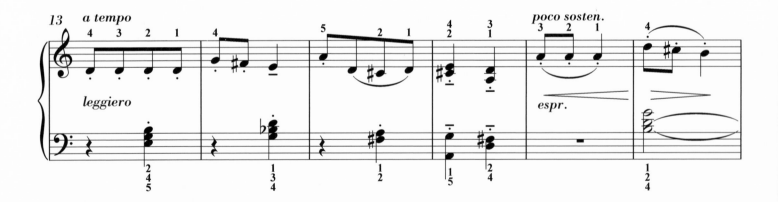

Fingerings are by the composer.

The Plaid Miss

from *Monsterpieces (and Others)*

William Bolcom

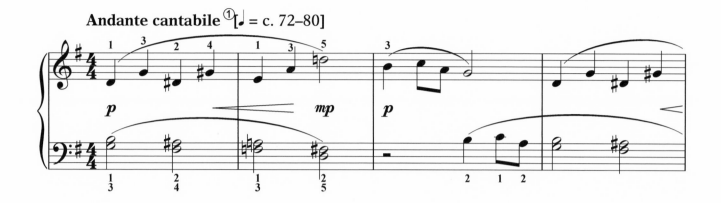

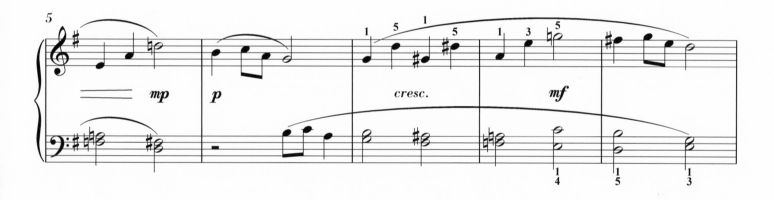

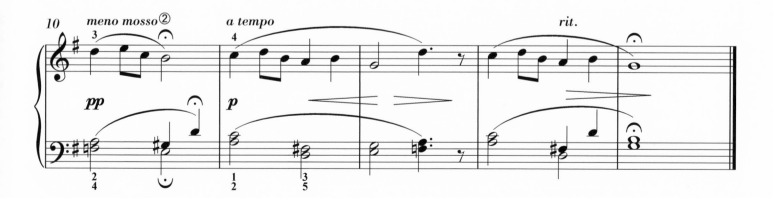

① *cantabile* = "singing"
② *meno mosso* = "slower"
Pedal is used sparingly in this piece, only for color. Try to make your left hand smooth as you can without using pedal.
Fingerings are by the composer.

The Missing Beat!

from *At the Piano*, Book 1

Morton Gould

Happy and fast Waltz time [♩. = c. 66–72]

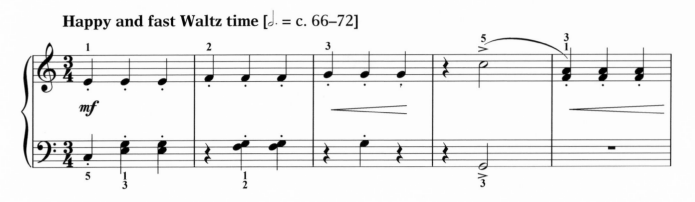

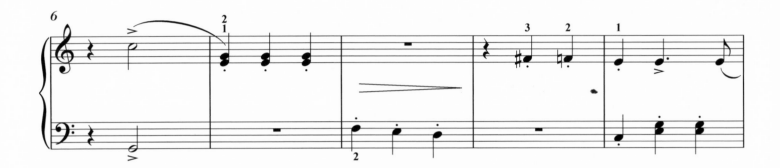

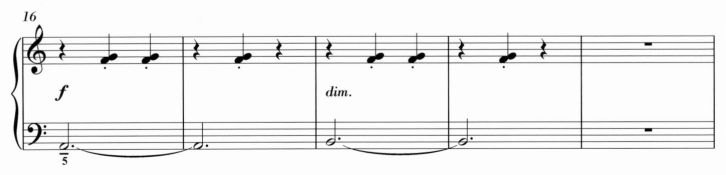

Fingerings are by the composer.

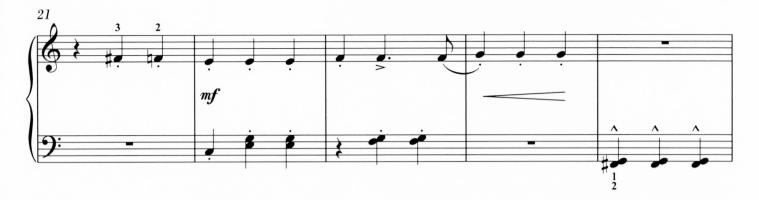

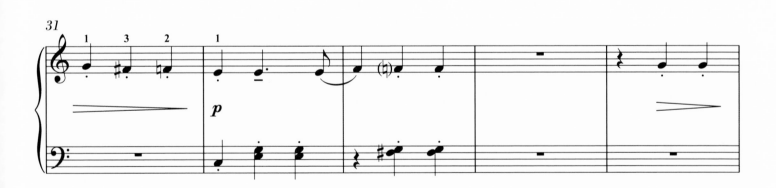

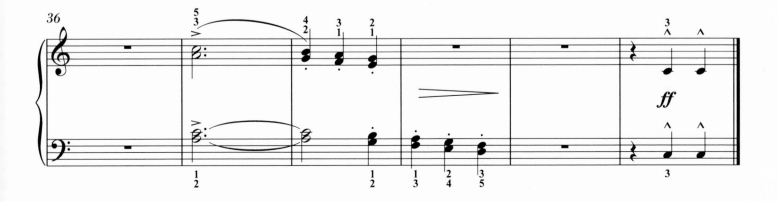

Loud and Soft
from *Ten for Deborah*

Morton Gould

Brightly [♩ = c. 180–200]

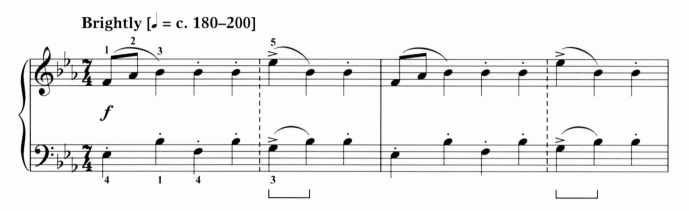

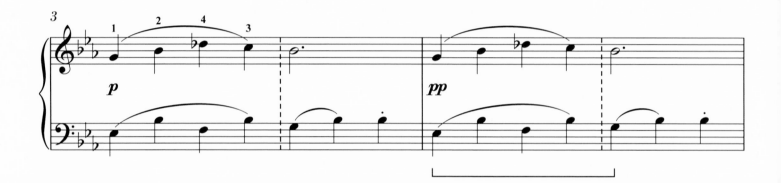

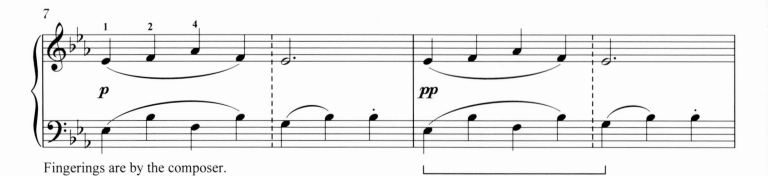

Fingerings are by the composer.

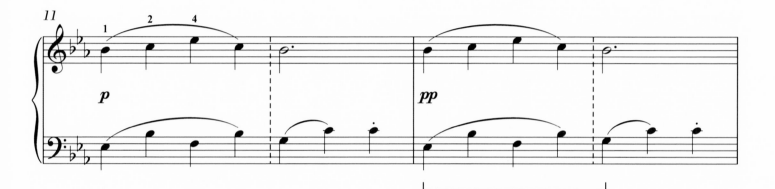

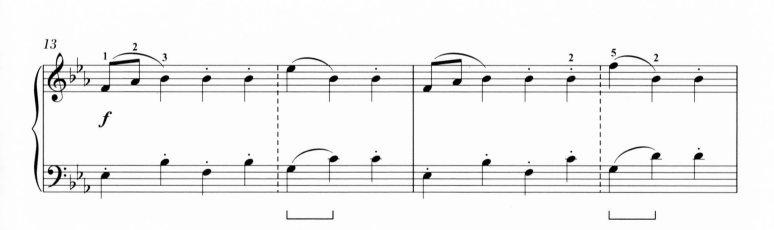

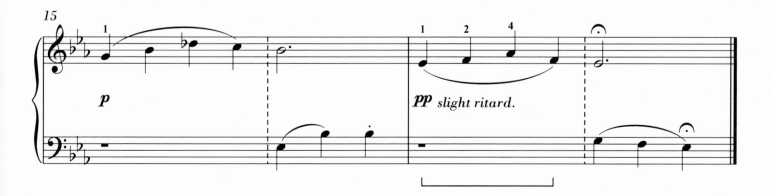

Sad Tale

from *Children's Notebook for Piano*

Dmitri Shostakovich
Op. 69, No. 5

(*L.H. crosses over*)

Fingerings are editorial suggestions.

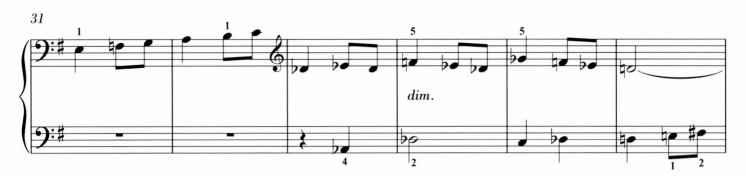

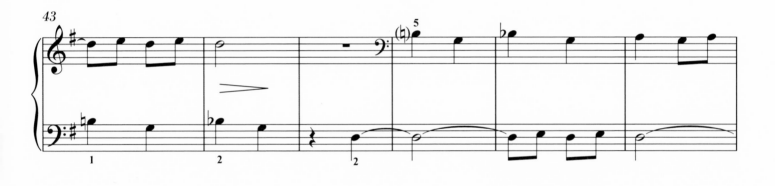

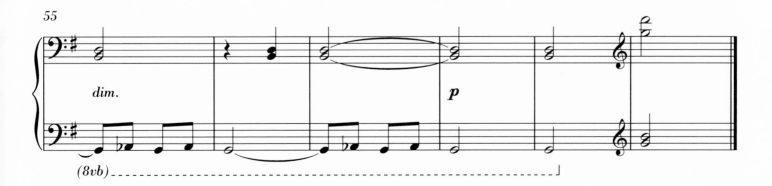

Merry Tale
from *Children's Notebook for Piano*

Dmitri Shostakovich
Op. 69, No. 4

Allegro [♩ = c. 112–120]

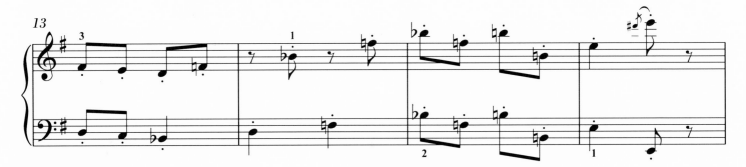

Fingerings are editorial suggestions.

The Shrew
from *35 Easy Pieces*

Dmitri Kabalevsky
Op. 89, No. 12

Allegro marcato [♩ = c. 120–132]

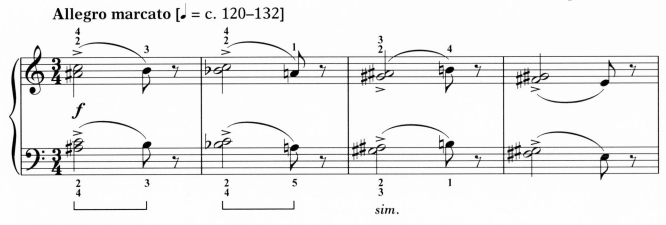

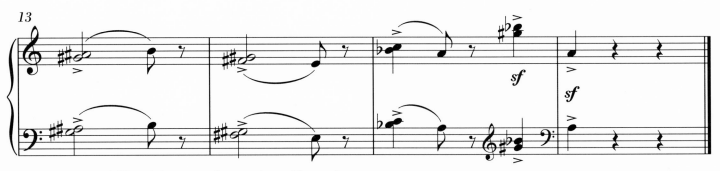

The composer deliberately uses enharmonic spellings of notes.
Fingerings are by the composer.

Badminton
from *Monsterpieces (and Others)*

William Bolcom

Pretend your two hands are two players. [any tempo is possible]

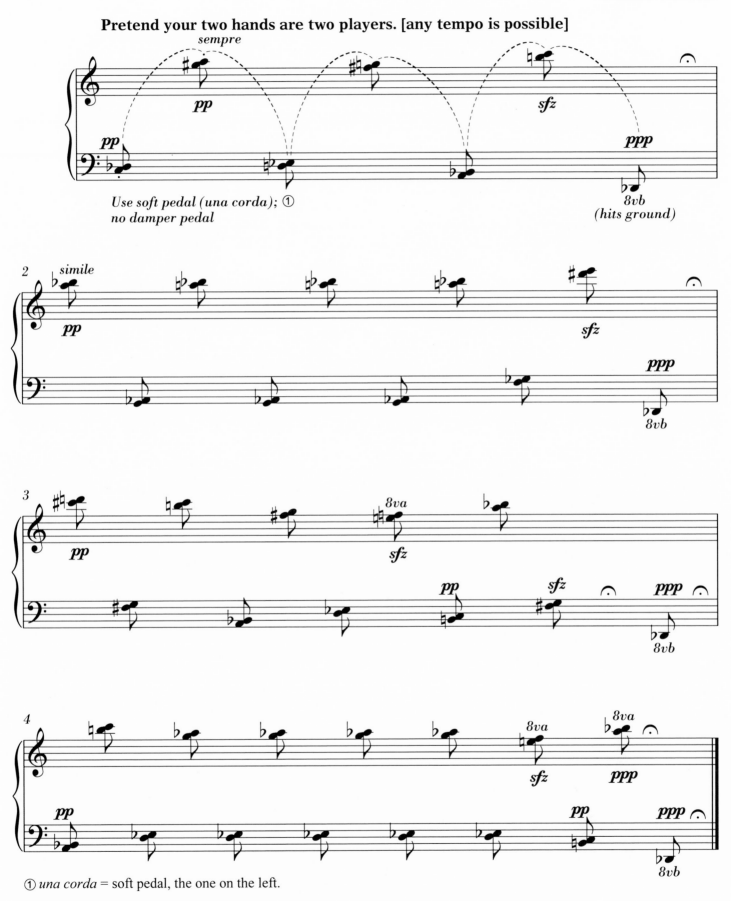

Use soft pedal (una corda); ①
no damper pedal

8vb
(hits ground)

① *una corda* = soft pedal, the one on the left.

Clowns
from *24 Pieces for Children*

Dmitri Kabalevsky
Op. 39, No. 20

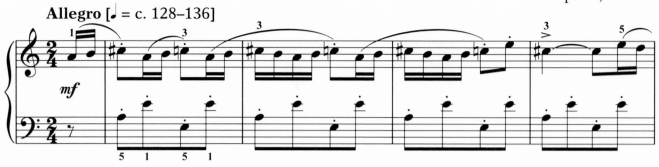

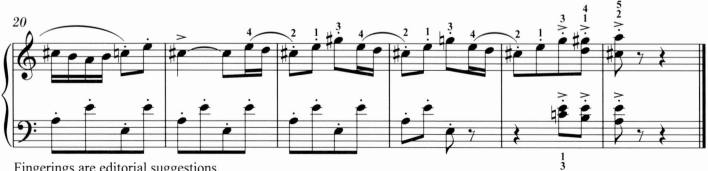

Fingerings are editorial suggestions.